𝓘𝓷

Irby

By F. Edward Butterworth

HERALD PUBLISHING HOUSE

Library of Congress Cataloging in Publication Data
Butterworth, F. Edward.
  Irby.

  1. Mundy, Irby. 2. Rodeos. I. Title.
GV1834.M86B87   791.8   74-28462
ISBN 0-8309-0143-4

Printed in the United States of America
by Herald Publishing House
Independence, Missouri

Dedicated to

JEWEL (WOODLEY) MUNDY
AND
DOROTHY (MUNDY) BROWN

Foreword

Irby Mundy was one of the most colorful characters of the Reorganization. A devoted husband and father at home, he was also a big brother to tens of thousands of adults and children in the public arena.

Such a rare person as Irby deserves a prominent place in the history of the church as one of the great personalities of our time.

The Author

Acknowledgments

*Special thanks to Mrs. Ellen Glatz
and Mrs. Lilly B. White of Chico,
California, to Gene Howard of
Cheyenne, Wyoming, and to the
Herald editorial staff.*

Oklahoma

$\mathcal{B}$efore I caught a glimpse of the familiar ten-gallon hat, cowboy boots, and friendly smile I knew it was Irby Mundy. His fire-engine red rig, the sharp whinny coming from beneath the dome-shaped canvas covering the truck bed, and the curb-scraping halt in front of the parsonage at Oklahoma City announced his arrival. Without a word the square-shouldered man dropped the tailgate on the pickup, backed down his famous horse, Sabe Dunn, and staked him square in the center of the church lawn. Furtively I glanced about to see how my neighbors were reacting to this since we were at Eleventh and Shartel near the heart of the city. Surely there were rules of some sort against grazing animals on the front lawn of a church.

"Don't worry, old Sabe Dunn is smarter than people...loves holy hay...needs water. Got a pail?"

I had to be alert to sort out the words as Irby fired them at me in his rapid, high-pitched, unpunctuated manner. If I got it right, Irby had asked for a bucket of water for his horse, so I scurried about to fetch it. When I returned Irby was gone. He had spotted some hay near a rabbit hutch across the street and had already negotiated the purchase of half a bale. Far from being unhappy about having a horse in the area, a small crowd of neighbors soon gathered to admire the animal and watch it graze. This was a pastoral scene not often witnessed in the city, and just watching it seemed to provide a certain therapy. In two days the rodeo at Claremore, Oklahoma, would begin. Here Irby was to appear in the calf-roping, bull-dogging, and steer-roping events as he had done for years.

"Old Irber," as many of his closest friends called him, was a true cowboy cast in the rare mold of the old West. His most striking physical feature was a huge nose set smack in the middle of a ruddy face. His thin lips, tightly drawn over a full set of natural teeth, curled up at the corners in a perpetual smile. His eyes—mere slits—sparkled as though he was peering into the sunrise.

"Where's the Erick kid?" Irby asked. "Like to palaver a spell before I mosey on." He had expected to find Merle Howard, but I had recently replaced Merle as pastor at Oklahoma City.

"Merle's not here anymore...moved to Midland, Michigan. You probably don't know me."

"Sure I know you...knew ye since ye were high as a mule's knee. Knew your father...used to run the Walnut Park Garage...fine mechanic...worked on Old Betsy here many a time. Warmed my boots at his fire waitin' for an overhaul and so forth and around.* Know your sister at Walnut Park—organist there. Mighty fine bunch of good eggs. Met you first in Truman Town...bad egg turned good."

I couldn't fault Irby on any of his information, except maybe his statement about the "bad egg turned good," since there were still debates in some quarters

---

*Irby used the phrase "and so forth and around" so often in his lingo it was difficult to follow his trend of thought. I have used it sparingly—for effect only.

Irby had a unique relationship with animals; they com-
municated. Perhaps that is why his horses were in such
demand at the rodeos.

Irby Mundy with his "covered wagon."

Four generations of the Mundy family posed: (left to right) Abbe, Irby, Dorothy Nell, and Barbara.

16

about how good the bad egg had turned out.

"Know your wife's folks even better," Irby continued, calling Lilly Raye by name. In his characteristic clip, however, her name came out "Liray." "Just came from Erick...visited B.A. and all the Saints there." Irby knew just about all the members and called most of them by name or, more often, by some nickname he had invented.

I was on the front row when the rodeo opened at Claremore that midsummer day in 1943. I wanted to see "Old Irber" in action. It was a beautiful day; filmy clouds edged with silver provided a welcome overcast since my seat was far from the cover that jutted out over the main pavilion. Irby had reserved a good seat for me close to the chutes where most of the action would take place. A faint breeze brought the aroma of old leather, sweat, and stable smells. Then the wind shifted and brought other scents—cheap perfume, beer, coffee, popcorn. I was not far from a hot dog stand, so I took advantage of the delay to satisfy my hunger. Usually Irby's wife and daughter worked in the concession stand, but they were not with him this trip.

Trumpets that had been blaring twenty strong fell silent just as I returned to my seat.

"Ladies and Gentlemen," a man's voice thundered over the raucous public address system. "Welcome to the annual rodeo at Claremore, Oklahoma. To get things started we present those zany clowns of renown, Janie and John." Instantly two outlandishly dressed clowns shuffled into the arena followed by a pair of nags with the dubious talents of stupidity and laziness. In spite of the efforts of the clowns, the quadrupeds refused to run, turn around, or even move their tails. The clowns pantomimed every trick the horses were supposed to perform, but still they stood in frozen pose, allowing the clowns to beat, push, and slap them. The cause seemed lost until a lively mule came rushing in from the opposite side of the arena. The quickened action turned the scattered ripple of applause into a thundering ovation. Bosomy Janie with the oversized shoes, proved to be an agile acrobat—obviously male. It was a good opening act.

Suddenly, before the formal introduction, a familiar figure astride his equally familiar mount burst onto the field. The applause and shouts were deafening.

"That world-famous movie star and renowned cowboy, Roy Rogers, and his horse Trigger." Roy had already made one complete circle of the arena standing in his stirrups and waving his white, broad-brimmed hat. The crowd was on its feet to a man. Trigger reared on his hind legs and danced about. I knew now why the amplifier had been turned up so high. At moments like this you could hardly hear the M.C. It was an exciting spectacle.

For fully ten minutes Roy Rogers circled the field, left, then entered again because the crowd refused to quit cheering.

A publicity picture taken in New York about 1942 shows Roy Rogers with his arms around Irby and Jewel Mundy.

Cowboys squatted in rows along the fence to await their turn at the first competition of the day which was to follow the grand entry.

For half an hour the program moved quickly as a procession of calf-ropers vied with each other. The event was won by an Oklahoma boy of eighteen. The runner-up from Texas was only two tenth seconds behind; he, too, was in his late teens.

"Ladies and Gentlemen. To close the calf-roping event, we present a man who wears a belt buckle marked Calf-Roping Champion of the World—Irby Mundy." Again the crowd was on its feet cheering.

Irby was shown at work in the steer roping competition by the photographer at the Pendleton, Oregon, Rodeo in 1946. (Photo by Devere Helfrich)

20

This photo taken around 1934 shows Irby roping a calf in Cheyenne. Irby always roped hatless (his trademark). He also used a large loop in his lariat although many other cowboys preferred to use a small loop.

Hugh Bennett (l.), Mickey McCrary (c.), and Irby (r.) take on a wild horse in Boston Gardens about 1940. Teamwork was required to get the horse saddled and ridden the required distance in the race. (Photo by Anthony F. Zilinsky)

Gene Howard, acting as Irby's assistant, threw open the chute, and out bounded a red-and-white calf. Irby, hatless and low in the saddle, taking care not to break the barrier, thundered out of the chute on Sabe Dunn with lariat spinning. It was a symphony of motion. Irby watched intently for that split second when he must throw the rope. Suddenly, like the paw of a cat, out shot Irby's hand and the loop went straight toward the head of the calf. With a practiced twist he sent the loop directly over the head of the calf. A quick jerk took the slack in perfect timing, and the calf was roped. When the rope left Irby's hand he pulled his rein, hollered "Ho," and Sabe Dunn went into his half-sitting, braking stop. Instantly the rope snapped taut. Irby had already left the saddle and was on the ground. Two steps and he was over the calf—flip, two loops of the piggin' string and Irby's hands flew up in the air.

The crowd roared. It was easy to see the difference between a champion and the competing amateurs. I could not follow all the action in that event, but re-creating it in my mind I recalled seeing Sabe Dunn's unvarying cadence, and the thick muscles rippling over his robust frame. He was the best trained horse I had ever seen. I could hardly believe it was the same animal I had seen grazing peacefully on the church lawn a few days earlier. In an unassuming manner Irby went to sit among the admiring amateurs. In spite of his rough occupation there was a softness in his fiber that made him lean toward the underprivileged and strugglers. Basically he was a man of simple habits and virtuous inclinations. No amount of coaxing could cause him to depart from his principles of moderation.

Irby's speech, often sprinkled with expletives, sometimes shocked his friends, but it was always sensible and spirited. People liked to be around Irby, and Irby liked to be around people.

"Old Irby was born in jail," Gene Howard told me as we talked together through the fence during the bulldogging event. "Plumb tuckered out the doctor to unwind Irby's fist from the umbilical cord the day he was born. Had a rope in his hands ever since. Before he was eight, the neighbors said, he'd roped every dog in the county that crossed his path."

"You say he was born in jail?" I asked.

"His father was the first sheriff of Childress County, Texas. The family lived in the second story of the jail at the time Irby was born."

Gene, a cowboy in his own right, often helped Irby at the rodeos in Oklahoma and Cheyenne. His job was to assist Irby in and out of the chutes and to care for the animals.

"Now to close the bulldogging event," the M.C. bellowed. "We present once again that world champion cowboy, Irby Mundy." The announcement had to be fast or it would have been drowned out by the roar of the crowd. Gene opened chute No. 1 and out charged a wild, red-eyed, frothing-at-the-mouth

Lined up for the photographer were the young Mundy brothers: Harry, seven; Henry, one; Claude, three; and Irby, five.

Father Harry and Mother Abbe (Perdue) Mundy joined the boys for a family portrait a few years later. Standing (l. to r.) Henry "Col," Irby "Coondog," Harry "Shike," and Claude "Boots."

A happy Irby displays the saddle he won in the wild cow milking contest at Madison Square Garden in New York in 1942. (Photo by Alexander Archer)

steer. Hugh Bennett hazed the animal while Irby, riding at the top of his speed, measured the steer, watching for his opening. Sabe's eyes protruded; obviously he considered this serious business. He could not know that it was all a game to the pleasure seekers sitting in the stands. Irby had drawn the wildest steer in the lot. Its fury was tenfold over the other animals that had previously entered the arena. There was usually a sense of frustration when one drew such an animal to dog before a critical audience, but a smile played on Irby's lips as he sped alongside the charging steer.

By some miracle of agility he was off Old Sabe, falling directly over the sharp horns of the animal. With practiced accuracy he grabbed the steer's horn and muzzle and with a mighty effort twisted the steer's neck toward the ground. Seven hundred pounds of animal flesh fell headlong into the dust. The whole operation took exactly 11.7 seconds.

"That's how Irby got hurt," Gene said. "A steer gored his right hand and pinned him to the ground a few years ago. Doctor said he'd never throw another one but you've just seen him do it." I had noticed that Irby's hand was misshapen a bit, but I supposed it was due to hurling the lariat.

It was a good show, and the crowd loved every minute of it. The women and children cheered as loudly as the men. Nothing marred the enjoyment except the discomfort which humidity occasions.

After the show I visited in Irby's bachelor quarters on the rodeo grounds. It was a tent filled with cowboy trappings—saddle, harness, spurs, and ropes of all kinds.

26

"When Jewel and Dorothy travel with me it doesn't look like this," he said, "but it's much easier this way." The place was not as bad as he indicated. In fact one end of the tent looked like a shoe store. There were several neat rows of cowboy boots lined up according to size and quality.

"I can fix you up with a good pair of boots," Irby said. "What do you say?"

"Never wear 'em," I replied, "but if you sold cowboy hats you'd have yourself a sale."

"No money in hats...got to be made of tooled leather to sell." Irby showed me the beautiful saddle he had won at Madison Square Garden in 1942. If it was not on one of his favorite horses he used it as a backrest or pillow in the tent—to keep it from being stolen.

Two days following the rodeo Irby visited our youth camp at Turner Falls. As soon as the sun went down, small night creatures raised their voices in throbbing unison, and the volume increased as the light faded. Flames of the campfire highlighted the happy faces of campers awaiting a cowboy tale of the West. Following a chorus of robust songs and hymns, Irby stretched his towering frame above his cross-legged listeners and began to speak.

He laid no claim to talents of public speaking, but on the theme for which he was renowned he was always in one of his keenest talking moods. Nor did he have any superiors in knowing how to sweep the chords of the human heart when speaking of the cowboy life.

He picked up the coil of rope that lay at his feet and whirled it over the heads of the campers. Then I introduced him, shook his hard-gripping hand, and went to sit on the rim of the charmed circle.

"Notorious Ed asked me to tell you about my cowboy life," he began. "I was born in a Texas jail but haven't been in one since. Finished the sixth grade at school, and my father sent me and my older brother Harry to business school in Fort Worth. Lasted only three weeks at that tomfoolery. Kept slipping off to the stockyards where there was some sense to life and so forth and around. Sat on the fence and looked the critters in the eye. Seems like I could talk to the animals, and they'd answer back—just a lot of bawlin' to most people, but I felt I could understand 'em. Moved to Shamrock, Texas, when I was seventeen. Started my own ranch—that was the life for me. Had trouble with coyotes though; bought four Russian wolfhounds that cleared up that problem pronto. Ranchin' is hard, but it's the best life in the world. Never met any dishonest cowboys...friendliest, most generous people in the world." Irby stopped for a moment, whirled the rope a few times, then let it drop to the ground. "Never saw anybody who could whirl a rope and palaver at the same time except Will Rogers...good friend of mine—big man in every way. No cowboy though...more of a politician and follies entertainer. Cowboys live in the saddle. Their life is one round of beaneries, grogshops, pawnshops, gambling dens, and so forth and around. Been in 'em all over the West. Met a lot of famous people. Used to smoke a big pipe crammed full of Prince Albert; then the Salvation Army got me—I mean the same Salvation Army Notorious Ed belongs to. Ordained me a deacon in 1925. 'Course I'd quit my smokin' and carousin' by then. Belonged to the Methodists before

Irby and his daughter Dorothy with their Russian wolf-hounds at the ranch near Shamrock, Texas (c. 1916).

that. One day my mother heard about a Latter Day Saint preacher comin' to the schoolhouse in Utleyville where we lived. Told her I'd take her once but not to expect me to go every night. Preacher was J. D. Curtis —finest man I know; slapped his brand on me that very first night. Never missed a night nor many since. My whole family and I were baptized at the end of the series." Irby stopped to ask how long he should talk. The clamor of the campers made a reply unnecessary.

"Cowpokin' was more fun than work. Usually started movin' the herds about the time the spring chickens were fryin' size. Winter grazin' on free range was over. It was roundup time—time to sort out the brands and see which ones the young calves would follow. Sometimes had to drive 'em a heap of miles. Drove 'em hard during the daytime so they wouldn't drift too far away at night. Cows are crazy critters; if they know each other, everything's peaceful, but mix a stranger in with them and they fight. Drive 'em straight down the range and most of 'em do fine, but there's always a few lookin' for a chance to break away and run off. Lot like us people. Never saw a dumb animal though. Meet him on his ground and he'll outwit you every time. In strange territory you got an even chance. Cows are cautious, too. They know when you cross a stream you're supposed to get wet; that's why they don't like bridges—not natural. Trying to drive cattle over a bridge invites trouble. Loose boards can cause a stampede. Tried to drive a short-haired cherry-red heifer over a rickety bridge once. . .still got scars from that.

"Best to start driving cattle before daylight—take advantage of the cool—then let 'em rest during the heat of the day. This gives the cowboys time to look after the sick or lame animals and so forth and around. Also have to chase down the wild ones that wander off. Had one once that refused to stay with the herd until the trail boss threw a rope around its neck, jerked its head two feet in the air, ran his hand eight inches up one nostril and cut through the cartilage into the other nostril, then pulled a rope through the slit and gave a few jerks on the line. Cow soon learned to stay with the herd. Boss just left the rope in the nostrils. Made her docile as a lamb. Finally he took the rope off. Just one of the tricks of the trade.

"Cow camp was an interesting place. Need three things for a good cow camp: water, grass, and wood to burn. Mud is the cowboys' enemy; bogs the cows down. Fire is another enemy. We'd never drive a herd into a field of long, dry grass. If fire broke out the cattle would be doomed—or stampede, which is almost as bad. Had to watch so the wind would blow the fire away from the camp if it started.

"There were usually twelve of us on a cattle roundup," Irby continued. "The trail boss was always out in front scouting for water and pasture and so forth and around. Two others rode point—which was up front in the direction the herd was moving. Behind 'em were two swing men, one on each side. Two flank riders followed near the rear of the herd. Usually took three men to ride drag behind the herd. Always had at least one wrangler who herded the extra horses and, of course, the chuck wagon man." Irby had asked me to set up a blackboard by the campfire and now I knew why as he began to draw a rough sketch of a typical cattle run.

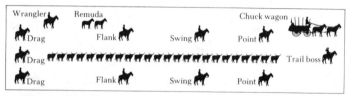

"Everything centers around the chuck wagon on a cattle run," Irby explained. "It goes as straight as the trail will allow—cowboys always drive the cattle forward but in toward the chuck wagon route." Again Irby drew a very good diagram to illustrate how the cowboys worked.

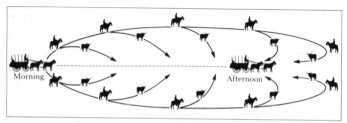

Irby looked up at the stars. "Well it's after nine o'clock so I'd better stop."

"How can you know what time it is by looking at the sky?" one of the youth asked.

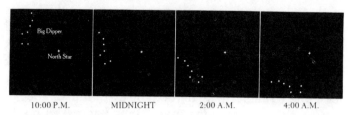

"See the North Star there?" Irby asked. "Now see the Big Dipper? When the handle of the dipper is straight up and down pointing north, it's between nine and

32

midnight. You can tell almost to the minute after a while as you learn the degrees the handle points and its relation to the North Star. When the dipper handle leans a few degrees to the left and the cup is opposite the North Star, it's midnight. At 2:00 a.m. the handle points northwest and the cup is at a forty-five-degree angle. At 4:00 a.m. the cup is flat and the handle points due west." Again Irby drew a series of diagrams to illustrate his point.

Because he was so unassuming, Irby was often seen as an ordinary man. A careful study of him, however, showed that he was made of the stuff of champions.

Irby's brother, H. H. Mundy (extreme left), served on the State Board of Agriculture of Oklahoma in 1941. He was a prominent rancher from Pawhuska.

He was actually a model of sobriety and self-discipline. His cowboy training had taught him this along with his genial but decisive manner. Split-second decisions were a part of his nature and no man in the world could top him in performance in this field during his prime. Yet Irby remained humble, approachable, considerate. He took time to write hundreds of people and often his lightest words had a way of bearing the weight of oracles. One of the few survivors of the old cowboy regimen, he saw no superiority of people because of their color, position, or rank. He talked as easily with royalty as with fellow cowhands; he was even welcome at women's meetings. He did not ask to dominate or to be applauded; he came to see if he could help. Now it was plain to me that he also knew how to entertain youth.

Truman Town

It was nearly eight months before I saw Irby again. This time it was in Independence, Missouri, where the 1944 World Conference was in progress at the Auditorium. I saw him enter the Conference Chamber dressed in his usual cowboy costume and walk the full length of the room to his reserved seat on the front row. His seat was marked with a cover bearing his name—the only personally marked seat in the entire Auditorium. As soon as he arrived at his place he tossed his hat to the first step on the rostrum, slicked down his hair, and turned to look around the chamber. When he sat down he pulled out a small brown paper bag and took out an apple. A few bites was all he wanted, but it satisfied him until he could have a full meal at the Laurel Club. To eat oranges—another of his favorite foods—he would usually go to the lower auditorium and take a seat in some isolated corner where he could suck the juice and not bother anyone.

Irby was best known for his interest in children. If he saw a child within a few rows of his seat he would pull a candy kiss from his bulging pockets and toss it to the child. It was a ceremony that many witnessed hundreds of times. Nearly all the children knew this lovable cowboy and many could call his real name, but most of them preferred to call him the "Candy

37

Irby went to the "feed bag" in the basement of the Auditorium during a break in activities. His sack of fruit provided food for the day.

Man." Irby not only attended World Conference but the *Messiah* performance. He was an expected part of both events. Thousands of people gathered at the Auditorium, yet in spite of the crowds, Irby was missed if he did not show up in his place.

I will long remember his visit to the women's quilting service at Walnut Park Church in 1948. He, too, was trying his hand at that meticulous task.

"This thread's a lot smaller than a lariat rope," he joked. "You'll probably have to take these stitches out after I leave and do them right."

"Nonsense, your work looks fine," the leader assured him.

"What are you going to do with this quilt?" Irby asked.

"Sell it and put the money in the building fund."

"How much do you get for a quilt like this?"

"We try to get around fifty dollars."

"Too cheap," Irby protested. "You should get twice that."

"Nobody will pay that much," one of the women said. "We've tried to get seventy-five dollars, but we usually have difficulty selling at that price."

"I'll give you one hundred dollars for this one," Irby offered. "This is good quality work....I like quality....I'll give it to my Jewel."

This was the Irby Mundy thousands learned to love.

Knowing that the quilt was to be for Irby's wife each woman decided to sew her name into a different block.

Those who received cards or letters from Irby Mundy—and this includes nearly everyone who wrote for the *Herald* or *Daily Bread*—never forgot it. He

39

always used green ink since he was born in Shamrock, Texas. The card, easily legible to the initiated, often started out with the heading "Mundy on Monday." His introduction usually followed one of two forms, "Dear Saint and Friend" or "Dear Good Writer." I have seen variations from these forms, such as "Dear Good Egg" or his usual greeting to me, "Notorious Ed, Truman City." Irby's daughter, Dorothy, told me his nicknames always fit, so I should probably explain the "Notorious Ed" designation lest I go down in history as a desperado. Irby saw me in a youth camp skit in which I was "Notorious Ed" in a two-gun shootout.

As the receiver of several of those colorful cards, I can truthfully say it made me feel good to know that someone had seen and appreciated my literary efforts.

It was not easy to decipher his cards, since he used his own brand of speed writing ("b" for "be," "2" as the prefix for "today," etc.). Something unique disappeared with the cessation of these communications.

"Roy Rogers is the most popular Hollywood star in the Islands," Apostle Clyde F. Ellis told Lilly Raye and me. We were at his home on River Boulevard in Independence in 1944 studying the Polynesian language in preparation for our first mission in the South Pacific. "I've seen pictures of Irby with Roy," Ellis continued. "It would be interesting if you could take some of those photos with you to show the natives." We followed through on this idea, and by return mail we received the following card, along with a packet of pictures and rodeo advertising:

Notorious Ed and New Bride, Truman Town—yes I
knew Roy R—pictures coming—roped with him in

Madison □ New York—most famous cowboy in the world—was stand-in for him in movies roping calves, steers, etc.—give Tahiti pardners big and small Old Irber's love.

The Ole Cowhand

One month after Lilly Raye and I arrived in the Islands I posted these pictures of Roy and Irby on the bulletin board at our Tarona headquarters building. Accompanying the pictures I wrote a short note explaining them. It was the most far-reaching note I had ever written, because for years after this notice appeared rumors were circulated about it. They ranged from Roy Rogers being a member of the "Sanito,"* to Roy Rogers being a personal friend of mine. All over Polynesia where I traveled I would meet these questions. Irby and I chuckled over this many times. I must hasten to add, however, that I had been in the Islands only one month before I published the note about the pictures. At any rate it gave me an opening and a conversation piece in places that otherwise might have been closed to me.

A few years later I received a letter from Irby while we were still in Tahiti. He was responding to my request that he tell the Polynesians something about cowboy life.

A cowboy is never lonely if he learns that nature is his friend. Cows, bulls (even the mean ones) can love and be loved. Birds, animals, even fish are ordained to serve, entertain, and sustain the cowboy, so we think of them as a part of our family just like brothers and

---

*"Saints Church," name for the RLDS church in French Polynesia.

sisters. Most of all good cowboys trust in the Great Spirit beyond the stars; he can see deep into our bones. That's the reason we must be honest and generous with our possessions. This is what binds men together...skin color makes no difference...twisted features cover beauty. The strong arm belongs also to the weak...riches belong to the struggling poor. This is the religion of the true cowboy who is a friend to all. Cowboys are part of every living action that strives to beautify the earth.

Colorado

Irby Mundy wore the trappings of the traditional cowboy, but he was a one-of-a-kind individualist. Praise was forever on his lips—a quality that endeared him to his friends and neighbors. With a jolly simplicity he refused to let others complicate his life. He possessed the brute strength to subdue any bully, but he was inclined toward docility. His generous nature, gallant bearing, and patriotism made him a first-rate citizen in every respect. His devotion to his family and friends was but an outward expression of what his religion meant to him.

"I'm on a big church run," he would say as he visited members in various parts of the country where he was rodeoing. These "runs" usually followed the same pattern: stock show in Denver in January, rodeo in Tucson in February, stock show in Fort Worth in March, rodeos in Montana, Wyoming, Idaho, Nebraska, Oklahoma, Kansas, Colorado, North and South Dakota, California, Washington, and Oregon from April to September. In October he was usually at Madison Square Garden in New York for the annual stock show and rodeo. In November he usually closed the season at the Boston Garden, then home to Shamrock, Texas, for December and part of January.

"Tell me about your cowboy friends, Irby," I coaxed. "So far I've heard only about those who went to Hollywood."

"The real cowboys who know how to punch, break, ride wild horses, and rope only go to Hollywood to stand in for the big stars," he began. "The best cowboys I ever worked with were Sabinal-Menoche and Old Dash*—both world champions." Irby was the third member of this famous triumvirate but he never mentioned the fact. These three men set records all over the United States. Usually when a record was set by one of them, the others hazed or assisted by riding alongside. No performer can achieve world record if the stage is not set properly by his assistant.

"Dash called me 'Coondog' because of the way I headed off the stock," Irby continued. "I called him 'Dash' 'cause he was fast. Came from Mangum, Oklahoma...good friend of Will Rogers. But old Sabinal was my closest friend. Best cowboy God ever made. Married a fine girl from Arizona, Josie McCuen—wonderful folks! Never argued much with him 'cause he was over six feet tall and strong as an ox...good personality...gentleman in every respect."

"Why do you call him 'Sabinal'?" I asked.

"Hugh and I met an old codger named Pat Tucker in Livingston, Montana. Funny little old man... usually wore a buckskin outfit...always singing a catchy tune. Hugh and I asked him to sing it for us, but the only words we could understand were 'Sabinal, Menoche, Fandango.' Whenever he'd see us he'd start singing those words, so Hugh and I called each other those names. If Hugh called me 'Sabinal,' I'd call him 'Menoche,' and so forth and around. Love to see old Tuck again. It was the way with us cowboys—always gave the others nicknames."

*Hugh Bennett and Ike Rude

46

Irby and his Jewel shown during a visit to Long Island in 1935. His prized champion buckle can be seen on his belt.

Friends Josie and Hugh Bennett at their ranch home in Falcon, Colorado, in 1954.

Pat Tucker, author of Riding the High Country, *is shown at Livingston, Montana, about 1934.*

Later I was able to ask Irby's daughter, Dorothy, about some of those nicknames.

"He called me 'Priss' during my younger years," she began. "Later this changed to 'Doss'—probably because when he would ask me my name when I was learning to talk I'd say it was 'Dossy Nell.' He called my daughter, Barbara, 'Mlam-Mlam.' This originated

48

from the fact that when she blew soap bubbles for him it made a sound of 'mlam-mlam.' And he called our James 'Doo.' This was the result of a conversation in which Dad asked James what he was doing, and the boy answered, 'I'm doing around.' Both of my children called their grandfather 'Pardner,' which pleased him very much. All of these nicknames stuck. Irby called his mother 'Coon,' but I have no idea how that originated. And he called his father 'Pappy.' He called all blondes 'brunette' and vice versa. Other nicknames he put on people included Rooster, Wasp, Snake, and Cactus. He called his nephew, James Barnard Mundy of Houston, 'Potty' because when he was a small child he had a little pot stomach. Irby's only other nephew, John Irby Mundy, was 'Young John.' He called his oldest brother 'Shike,' his second brother 'Boots,' and his youngest brother 'Col.' These names stuck with them all their lives."

"What about the horses you've owned?" I asked Irby. "You must have had some good ones in your day."

"My favorite was Happy, a bay quarter horse. Bought him in Springfield, Colorado, around 1923... carried the brand 'Quarter Circle 44' on his left hip. I won Patches in a horse race. Some young fellow near

Utleyville had a quarter horse—called him that cause he could run very fast for a quarter of a mile. Wanted to match in a race with old Happy. Held him off for a long time by saying it wouldn't be fair 'cause no horse in the country could outrun Happy in a quarter mile race. The fellow kept after me so finally I said, 'If you just feel like you've got to race Patches against Happy, I'll run that race, but the winner gets the other horse.' It was agreed, and we raced at Pritchett, Colorado. Happy won that race by a country mile. Had another fine quarter horse, 'Rock,' named for the town where he was purchased—Red Rock, Oklahoma.

Irby's rodeo horses, Happy (foreground) and Patches.

"These three horses shared the same stalls, and Happy and Patches rode side by side in the trailer. Made a good bulldogging team. But I used Rock for roping only. Happy was a good roping horse too. Won hundreds of dollars with my horses. Other cowboys would use them for bulldogging and roping events, and if they won, I got a third for the use of the horses. I always rode Happy and Patches in the relay races. I was too heavy to be a good race rider, but they were almost unbeatable.

"Old Happy dropped dead of a heart attack at Colfax, Washington, back in 1940 while I was riding him hazing a steer for Ike Rude. He just stumbled and dropped. Rock died in Calgary—got sleeping sickness from mosquito bites. Sold Patches to Ray Mavity, a cowboy from Montana. All my horses were real pets. Losing 'em was like losin' part of the family.

"Had some good horses when I worked for the Mill Iron Ranch near Shamrock, Texas," Irby continued. "The Continental Land and Cattle Company owned this ranch—combined it with the Rocking Chair Ranch about 1895. The Ox and Shoe-Nail Ranches bordered Mill Iron on the east; Shoe-Bar and Diamond Nail on the north; and Matador spread along the west and south. Worked for all of 'em at one time or another...all honest outfits. Used to go to Montana where the Mill Iron leased a ranch. That's where they got their wild horses. I used to catch them and bring 'em to Texas."

No wonder he was such a good rodeo performer. Competing in the arena was child's play after roping in the wilds.

I shall never forget Irby's colorful lingo. He called washday Sudsville and described his food in phrases like son-of-a-gun stew, vinegar pie, hush puppies, and ash cakes. He always wanted to be a cook during the cattle runs, not because he was particularly skilled in the culinary arts but because cooks made ten dollars a day more than cowboys.

Irby's world championship belt buckle was his proudest possession—and rightly so. It had a personalized likeness of him and his horse Happy—an action shot of Irby roping a calf. All of this was in raised gold against a silver background. It contained his name along with the words "World Champion Calf Roper, 1934." On the back was the inscription: "Presented to Irby D. Mundy of Utleyville, Colorado, world's champion calf roper and fourth in the world's all-around cowboys championship in 1934, by Maxwell McNutt, President of Rodeo Cowboy Association." In 1942 Irby captured first prize in the wild cow-milking event and added still another championship trophy to his mementos.

Irby and Roy Rogers are shown again following the 1942 World's Championship Rodeo.

Wyoming

Cheyenne was Gene Howard's adopted home and no other city was in the competition. When Irby came to Cheyenne, Gene was his constant companion and most ardent admirer.

"What can you tell me about Irby's life in Cheyenne?" I asked Gene.

"Irby Mundy was one of the group of ranch-reared, ranch-trained cowboys who laid the foundation for professional rodeo as it is known today," he began. "They were genuine cowboys—products of the cattle and ranch industry that developed in the grassy plains region of the western states. With the passing of the buffalo herds large areas of grasslands were made available for ranching activities. Present-day rodeo events evolved from the everyday life of the working cowboy—with the exception of steer wrestling or bulldogging. Early-day rodeos were largely local or small area events. Professional rodeo became a national sport in the 1920s with the advent of reliable trucks and paved highways.

"Certain of these early-day cowboys found life in rodeo competition to their liking and made it their way to earn a livelihood. Irby was one of this group. He had the natural ability to win enough prize money to assure a good living.

"For professional cowboys all roads lead to Cheyenne—the 'Mecca' of rodeo—during Frontier

Days, the last week in July. It is not only one of the oldest rodeos in the United States but features perhaps the largest and best arena, excellent climate, and the biggest purse in rodeo.

"Irby first came to Cheyenne in the 1920s. He was a tough competitor during his prime years, between the two World Wars. Anyone who competes in the timed events—calf-roping, single steer roping, and bull-dogging—is dependent on fast, well-trained horses. Irby always had one or more of these fine animals. Probably no better horse ever competed in rodeo than Happy.

"Competing with other cowboys required a high degree of coordination, strength, and judgment. Irby learned to judge steers and calves just by looking at them in the catch pen or in the first round of competition. This skill helped him to win his share of the purses. He had another source of income too. Frequently he would haul as many as four horses and rent them to other cowboys for a share of their winnings. Sometimes when a cowboy had hard luck at a previous rodeo Irb would pay his entry fee for the amount back and a percentage of his winnings. Occasionally, of course, he lost his investment, but this didn't happen often.

"Basically, he had good judgment as well as ability in many areas or he could never have made a success of the rodeo way of life. About 1939 when the old-time relay races were abandoned Irb obtained a relay race saddle with a shaped cinch for use in the wild horse race. This event required a team of three men to ear down, hold, saddle, and ride a wild, unbroken horse around the race track to win. That relay saddle when

58

Irby mounted on Happy hazed a steer for Jim Irwin who rode Patches at the Kiowa Rodeo.

Shorty Creede bulldogs off Patches while Irb hazes on Buck.

thrown on a wild horse would by spring action have the cinch at the right place, ready to fasten immediately, which saved several seconds time in saddling. That year Irby and the two men on his team were the big winners in wild horse racing at Cheyenne.

"Although Irby won more money in calf roping and became a world champion in that event, his favorite rodeo event was single-steer roping. Although this was banned in many states, it was a very necessary skill in the ranch days of the old West. At that time branded steer calves were turned loose on the open range until they were three or four years old. It took a real cowboy to round up and corral these wild steers. Irby was one of these good hands. Building a large loop and swinging slowly, he would seldom miss a catch. Later competitors found that using a smaller loop and a fast swing resulted in a quicker tie. However, for many years Irb won most of the roping events."

"Is rodeo life as colorful as it appears?" I asked Gene.

"It's strenuous, requiring forty or fifty thousand miles of travel a year. Sometimes Irby would finish a rodeo one afternoon or evening and drive all night to reach another four or five hundred miles away. He would be there in time for the afternoon performance the next day. A typical July schedule would include ten days at Calgary, Alberta; three days in Sheridan, Wyoming; five days in Ogden, Utah; seven days here in Cheyenne; and three days at Boulder or Monte Vista, Colorado. His yearly schedule would start in January and end in early December and would cover rodeos from California to New York and from Calgary to south Texas. He knew more people in isolated areas than anyone else in the church. He also was well-known in show business in the areas that concerned the old West, horses, cattle, rodeo, and ranching.

"Irby led a clean life and was not a slave to any bad habits. He was fond of watermelons in hot weather and often came to Cheyenne with six or eight large melons—enough to last the week of Frontier Days.

"In his later years when his rodeo days were over he would go to the supermarkets and buy day-old bread and pastries. He would get two or three pickup loads per week and drive to the poorer sections of town and give it all away to the needy. He also went to Woolworths and bought candy kisses in hundred-pound bags."

"Could you understand Irby's lingo?" I asked.

"Certain of his comments were as typical of Irby as his letters and postcards. Some of his sayings that I remember are 'He's runnin' over dollars lookin' for quarters,' 'Put first things first,' 'When a man marries a good woman, he's got somethin'; and when he marries the other kind, he's still got somethin'.'"

"Did you know Irby's wife?"

"Yes, Jewell traveled with him on the circuit and was known and respected in the rodeo world. They always came to Cheyenne in pickups pulling horse trailers; here they camped on the rodeo grounds. At one time she said that they had been married for over thirty years and she had not unpacked her housekeeping things yet. Irb would never stay in anyone's home during his rodeo years. He would pay his entry fees in one or more events and spend several hours daily in

61

practice or in actual competition. While on the circuit he contacted church people and would get them free tickets to the rodeo. He didn't want his friends to buy tickets when he could give them free ones.

"Irby Mundy was an independent, generous man of action, the like of which we will not see again. Many people both in the church and out gained inspiration from personal contact with him."

Irb's Daughter Reminisces

A proud father, Irby poses with daughter Dorothy Nell.

"I'm Irby's only child," Dorothy Nell Brown wrote to me in 1973. "He never wanted me to call him Daddy or Papa. Instead, he taught me to call him 'Old Irber' which I did during my young life. Later I called him 'Irb.'

"He usually carried candy kisses in his pockets for the children, but he occasionally approached some mother and asked, 'Honey, may I give you a kiss?' He would then hand her a candy kiss. This was his way of joking.

"He taught me many things but the greatest, I think, was to be honest and generous. He lived by this code and taught others to do the same.

"My father was of pioneer stock. His father Harry Mundy and his mother Abbe Perdue traveled by covered wagon from Alabama in 1875. They met near Decatur, Texas, and were married in 1885. Shortly thereafter they moved to west Texas where he became the first sheriff of Childress County in 1887. Their living quarters were in the second story of the jail; here Irby Dunklin was born November 28, 1889. He was named for a prominent Texas lawyer and friend of the family. His early years were spent in Childress where I suppose he did all the things most young boys do. He talked of having a rope in his hands since childhood. Around 1906 the family moved to Shamrock, Texas,

65

where Irby worked for a few months on neighboring ranches. He didn't like working for wages, so at an early age—seventeen or so—he started buying and selling cattle. In 1911 he was married to Jewel Woodley. They spent their first year of marriage near Canadian, Texas, where he summered cattle. Later they moved back into Shamrock and built a new home. They lived there only a few months, then moved to a ranch southeast of Shamrock. They always had the latchstring out, and many old cowboy friends made their home a 'stomping ground.'

The first home of Irby and Jewel Mundy was built in Shamrock, Texas, around 1914.

"In 1917 Irby made a trip to Washington State and to Colorado looking for land to buy. He finally decided on a ranch eighty miles southwest of Lamar, Colorado, near Utleyville, which consisted of a country store and post office. While the land was good, the living quarters left much to be desired. For five years home was a one-room frame house; then a one-room dugout was added. My paternal grandparents and another family from Shamrock also moved to the Utleyville area, settling about five miles away. Although life was crude by present-day standards, those were happy years.

"My father owned one of the few Model T Fords in the vicinity, and in 1918 during the flu epidemic it was put to good use taking people to the doctor in Springfield. He himself became very ill with flu and almost lost his life. Only the good nursing care of his wife and mother pulled him through. There were few forms of entertainment except school affairs, box suppers, and picnics in the summer. One of the Mundys' favorite pastimes was the Saturday night dances at McArthur's Ranch about fifteen miles away. Sometimes they went in the car; other times they took a horse and buggy. These dances were held in the sheep-shearing sheds on the ranch, and people drove for miles around to attend them.

"In 1923 Irby and his family were baptized in a stock tank by J. D. Curtis. At that time there was only one church family near Utleyville—the Webbs. However, several others were baptized at the same service, and these Saints marked the beginning of the congregation there. Meetings were held first in the schoolhouse; then a few years later a church was built

67

Bruce E. Brown (l.), F. Henry Edwards (r.), and Irby were the three men who organized the branch at Utleyville.

F. Henry Edwards after Irby turned him into a cowboy.

68

at Utleyville. The branch was organized by Bruce E. Brown, president of Eastern Colorado District, and F. Henry Edwards. The Mundy home was always the stopping place for visiting church people, and I can remember how worried my mother was at the prospect of Brother Edwards coming to our crude house. We loved him because he was so humble and wonderful. My father had a great time putting western clothes on Brother Edwards, then posing him on a horse and taking his picture with a rope in his hand (the other end of the rope was tied to an already roped-down calf).

"Irby was enthusiastic over his conversion and wanted to share the good news with all his neighbors. He spent hours telling them the gospel story and also assumed the task of keeping the little schoolhouse neat and clean for all the services, since he had been ordained. Each Sunday we would go an hour early so that he could clean and arrange the seats for the services to follow.

Potato Butte School was the first RLDS meetinghouse in Utleyville, Colorado. The Mundys heard the gospel here in 1923 through J. D. Curtis.

"He always said that his pocketbook was converted along with him, and over his lifetime he gave thousands of dollars to the church. He attended his first Conference in 1925 and never missed a session until his last two years of life. Many times he took a truckload of Saints from Colorado and Oklahoma to Conference. He liked to tell of his love for Frederick M. Smith and of his respect for him as a prophet. Their friendship was a highlight of his life.

"Around 1927 things got rough financially, so Irby began going to small rodeos in the neighboring states of Kansas and Oklahoma. He always entered the calf roping event. This was one thing he had done all his life and he knew how to do it expertly. He was a consistent winner in these contests. He also did some bulldogging until his right hand was seriously injured when a steer fell on him. The muscles, tendons, and skin from the back of his hand were torn loose, and blood poisoning set in. He was hospitalized in Lamar, Colorado, for nearly a month, and the doctor told him he would never have the use of his hand again, but my father was not one to give up. For months he constantly squeezed a small rubber ball to help restore movement and flexibility and strength in his hand. The injury left some impairment but he went on to rope his way to a world championship and win over $3,300 dollars in one week.

"During the Great Depression he lost everything he had, so he started out in earnest to make his living by following the rodeos. This continued for eighteen years. He appeared in shows in many different states, ending every season at Madison Square Garden and the Boston Garden. It was a hard life, but he made a

70

Irby (r.) was among the winners in the bulldogging contest at the Coldwater, Kansas, rodeo in 1926. This was the first time he competed in that rodeo.

Ready to hit the rodeo circuit for the first time (1926), Irby checks his horse Blue with the help of a young nephew.

good living at it and contributed regularly to the church. We usually spent December and January in Shamrock and it was there we met Brother and Sister B. A. Howard. That meeting resulted in a long and valued friendship.

"Regardless of where we were, we always managed to find Saints and worship with them on Sundays or at any possible meeting. Many times my father would seek out isolated Saints and visit with them, if for only a few minutes.

"Irby had a heart as big as the outdoors he loved. Never would he pass up anyone in trouble. During the Depression years when so many people were hitchhiking, he 'cleaned up the roads' as he called it, picking up as many as his rig would hold. When he saw someone in trouble along the roadside, he'd stop, drag out the log chain which he always carried for that purpose, hook on the front of the car and pull it to the next town or where help was available. I remember one time in the wide-open spaces of Wyoming, he pulled a car back in the opposite direction fifty miles to a town. This cost him several precious hours between rodeos. Many times he and his cowboy friends would have to drive day and night to get to the next rodeo on time. In all his years of travel, however, he never had a serious accident on the highway.

"After retirement, he 'churched' in earnest and his red truck was a familiar sight all over the country. He loved to go to reunions and district conferences in the Southwest, and his circle of friends continued to grow. He was especially interested in Boys Ranch at La Junta, Colorado, and spent many hours there talking with the boys. He entertained busloads of them with

Dorothy Nell and her dad are shown in Independence in 1946.

Granddaughter Barbara perched atop Sabe, another famous roping horse belonging to Irby.

73

The Mundy home in Colorado Springs, Colorado.

A 1967 photo shows Irby with his fire engine red pickup loaded for another trip. (Photo by James Welch)

74

picnics at his home, and every year he took twenty-five or thirty of them to the rodeo in Penrose Stadium at Colorado Springs.

"Irby entered into many church-related activities in Colorado Springs, such as musicals. He attended services in other churches when there was no service in his own. In so doing he made many nonmenber friends from bank presidents to shoeshine boys.

"Irby always made it a point to attend the rehearsals of Handel's *Messiah* in Independence, Missouri, and was always on the front row at the presentations. He was proud of his front-row seat at General Conferences, and he treasured the chairback cover with his name on it for many years. It was on his wheelchair during his last days.

"He spent countless hours working on the Colorado Springs church when it was being built. He and three or four other men were usually the first to arrive and the last to leave during construction. He was willing to work at any hard job and was always on hand with his truck to do hauling. A physically strong man, he daily thanked God for his good health. In prayer services his remarks always included, 'I'm thankful for good health...never an ache or pain.'

"Irby always dressed in western clothes, including boots and a Stetson hat. I think he owned only one pair of regular shoes in his adult life. Among his proudest possessions was a 7X beaver Stetson given to him in the last year of his life by his best friend, Hugh Bennett, a rancher and ex-rodeo contestant of Falcon, Colorado.

"In 1934 he was declared World's Champion Calf Roper by the Rodeo Cowboys Association, and until his death he wore his trophy belt buckle. In 1942 he won the Wild Cow Milking Contest in Madison Square Garden and, in addition to his prize money, he was presented a beautifully tooled personal saddle. He was a good friend of Roy Rogers, and one of his treasures was a picture taken with Roy in New York."

Irby as he is remembered . . . tall in the saddle of a great horse.

I Remember Irby

It would be inappropriate to end the account of such an extraordinary life as Irby Mundy's with a description of his declining years.* To the enrichment of these pages I am adding a number of experiences and reminiscences sent to me by friends who knew him best.

FROM ROY CHEVILLE

Irby always sat on the front row, a little to one side, when I conducted prayer services at the Colorado Springs Reunion. I don't recall that he ever testified or prayed during these meetings, but it helped me to know that he was there. After one of the services he said to me, "That was the best damned prayer meeting I ever attended."

Despite his expletives and sometimes eccentric activities, Irby was not disrespectful. One Saturday I went into the Conference Chamber of the Auditorium as the orchestra was getting ready for rehearsal for the *Messiah*. The soprano soloist from Chicago was getting

---

*Irby Mundy died March 25, 1973, at Shamrock, Texas. He was buried in the Evergreen Cemetery at Colorado Springs, Colorado, on what would have been the Mundys' sixty-second wedding anniversary.

(Author's note: It was Roy Cheville who labeled Irby's characteristic chatter "Mundianese.")

ready to sing "I Know That My Redeemer Liveth," when Irby came in and sat down on the front row. He got an apple out of his pocket and started peeling it. He was about half through the peeling process when the soloist started to sing. He put the apple on his knife and held it there, refraining from eating while the soloist sang. When she had finished, he resumed eating. I couldn't help thinking that this was a different devotional center than she had ever had before.

I remember another time at Romoca Campgrounds at a gathering of patriarchs, the apostle, and the district presidents. Irby came, too. He did not eat or sleep with us (he stayed in his own auto trailer) but he attended all the meetings because, as he put it, "It's just good to be here with you boys."

I don't know how much Irby sang or how he sang, but one time when I was leading the singing he showed more interest than usual. We were really singing the gospel, and the Saints were responding. After the meeting he said to me, "You sing as if you mean it, and you do."

Once while I was traveling with Irby from his home toward Independence, I asked him about his itinerary. He replied, "I really don't have any. I start out and on the way I get an idea that might draw me off the track if I had a course. On the way I remember somebody who needs a friend or a visit, so I turn in that direction."

Irby always dressed in cowboy clothes. When I asked him if he slept with his boots on he replied, "I've never thought about that, but I think I take them off at night."

He once said, "I manage the best I can to get wherever the Saints have a roundup on Sunday morning; then I go to the rodeo in the afternoon." This was the Irby Mundy I knew.

FROM DON CHESWORTH

Irby attended nearly every church function held at Romoca Lodge in Colorado. He loved to make coffee and serve it to us. I liked him very much...probably because it was obvious he loved people.

His favorite "traveling foods" were oranges and hard-boiled eggs. I recall that he used to fill his truck with bakery goods and drive to the Auditorium at Independence. Members of the entire Auditorium staff were free to take what they wanted—no charge. It was typical of Irby's generosity.

FROM WARD HOUGAS

I became acquainted with Irby in the early fifties. He lived in Utleyville in the dirt-storm area seventy miles from the nearest railroad. Most of the people lived in two- or three-room dugouts, and it was not uncommon for them to find rattlesnakes in these half-underground dwellings.

The church was more like a shed with a few plain benches and an organ. At night the cattle would come in off the plains and crowd around the building. It was all I could do to make the forty parishioners hear me when the bawling range cattle thumped their tails against the building as they swatted flies.

Irby often came to my office in Denver when I was district president to talk about the church and its people. He had a deep sympathy for the needy and often filled his pickup with day-old bread to deliver to them.

He was a true deacon. He was not just there when the doors opened; he opened the doors before anyone else got there. He kept the place clean and warm and saw that the hymnbooks were distributed evenly.

When we had a church dinner, he was in charge of hymnbooks and garbage. He liked to sing, and he liked to eat, and he was quite willing to assume responsibility for the work involved with both functions.

In later years Irby told me he was changing from "rodeo" to "toe-deo." He was having trouble keeping up with the fast pace of rodeoing so he went to selling cowboy boots. And he did well at it.

Irby Mundy was Irby, Monday through Sunday—always the same beautiful person, a blessing to everyone he met.

FROM GEORGE NJEIM

My first acquaintance with Irby was in 1940 when I was preaching the Campus series at Independence. He was always concerned with people, and on this one occasion he wanted me to administer to a friend of his. At the appointed time I met him in front of the Auditorium and proceeded to the home of the sick friend. Upon reaching the house I asked Irby to give me a few details about the sick person so I could prepare myself. He told me that the friend was Sadie Katskowsky, who was converted to the church in Colorado at the time Irby and the Webbs were converted. He said that she had tuberculosis of the blood. Sadie was a regular contributor to the *Herald*, and I knew her through her writing.

While visiting with her I expressed my sympathy. She was very cheerful. "Well, Brother Njeim, I asked for it, and God gave it to me." "What a horrible thing to say!" I exclaimed. Her answer was the story of her conversion. She was a young woman when the gospel reached her, and in appreciation for what God did for her at that time she promised to dedicate herself for his service and the service of humanity. The question which arose in her mind was, "What can I do to prepare myself for this service?" She decided to become a teacher. After graduation she found a job; then came her disappointment. She had figured on adding another R to the regular three—religion. When the school trustees informed her they wanted the fourth R out, Sadie was very disappointed. She tried another school, and the story was the same. After that she decided to become a registered nurse. But here again she was disappointed. The sick listen to the word of God when they are sick, but once they recover they usually go back to their old ways.

The only way left for Sadie now was to ask God for guidance, and she did. When she contracted tuberculosis it seemed to her the answer to prayer. When I protested this, she began to explain. She had a lovely home, and her husband had a properous plumbing business. Although she was bedfast she said, "God gave me a good mind, and blessed me with a rich spirit. I put my typewriter on this portable bed table and write. The articles go to the *Herald*." Then she pulled a drawer from a nearby filing cabinet and said, "All of these letters are from people who have read my articles and have been brought nearer to God as the result." I noticed that during the conversation Irby's eyes were moist.

After the administration, when we were in his truck going back to the Auditorium, I asked, "Irby, who ministered to whom? Did we minister to Sadie, or did Sadie minister to us?" There was no hiding his tears as he answered, "She always ministers to those who hear her."

This was Sadie's story, but it was Irby's story as well. Here I was riding with a cowboy (and cowboys are known for their toughness) who was the most loving and caring person I knew.

On another occasion I was preaching a series in the Auditorium which was advertised heavily. Irby was in Colorado, but he was thinking of me. Assisting with the music was Frank Hunter. One morning I found a postcard in the mail addressed to

> George Njeim, one good egg, and
> Frank Hunter, another good egg,
> Truman Town
>
> Thinking of you two.
> Truman town needs eggs like you.

> Irby

Later I discovered that Frank Hunter received a similar card. This was Irby. He would not allow a moment to pass by if he could encourage anyone in the work of the gospel.

FROM ALFRED H. YALE

The first time I recall seeing Irby Mundy was at the World Conference of 1950. This tall cowboy, dressed to suit the part, took his place in a seat on the front row and was there for every session.

My wife, the former Miriam Winholtz of Ogden, Utah, pointed him out and said that he was a world champion in the rodeo circuit. She recalled that he used to come to Ogden for the rodeo each year, and she and her family often were invited to visit the Mundys while they were camped on the rodeo grounds.

I never saw Irby without some candy in his pocket for the children. My daughters were frequent recipients of his generosity.

I accepted church appointment that Conference (1950) and from then on, for many years, I received cards from Irby, always addressed to "Alfred Yale, a Good Egg." Every time one of my articles would appear in the *Herald* I could count on a card from Irby with some compliment about the feature.

While we were in the Tulsa District, Irby often appeared unexpectedly at a church service, priesthood gathering, etc. I learned quickly not to stand too close beside Irby for he had the disconcerting habit of punctuating his comments with a quick jab of his elbow to my ribs.

In his later years, when I visited the Colorado Springs church where our oldest daughter and her family attended, I would be greeted as a long-lost friend. Irby would insist that we come out to his truck where he would hand us a sack of bread and sweetrolls. He would make up dozens of such sacks and distribute them to members and friends on Sunday. It was his way of sharing.

Irby had a sense of independence which would not let him impose on friends. He preferred to eat an apple to imposing on a friend for a meal. He preferred to sleep in his bedroll in the back of his truck to imposing on someone for a bed. But he was proud of his wide range of friends across the country.

Irby was a man of simple but deep faith. Points of theology did not trouble him. He knew what God had done in his life. He moved unassumingly among the Saints, but those who knew him recognized him as a man of God who rode tall in the saddle.

FROM WAYNE UPDIKE

Although I met Irby Mundy in the 1940s when he visited his daughter in Kansas City and spoke with him briefly on various occasions when he attended World Conferences in Independence, my major association with him was during the years between 1967 and his death in 1973. These occasions took place at Romoca, a lodge at Palmer Lake, Colorado, and in the church at Colorado Springs. I also visited him in his home in Colorado Springs.

Irby attended most of the retreats and reunions held at Romoca. He came with his pickup loaded with bread, cakes, and rolls that had been given to him by a bakery or grocery store. These he distributed to the poor. He always refused to eat with the campers, preferring to take care of his own needs from the supply in his truck. He slept in the attic, and took great pride in always being available to help the ladies with their luggage. He considered it his personal responsibility to keep the fire going in the fireplace in the lodge and always filled the woodbox at the close of each camp. He liked to tell of his trips to Independence, usually referring to the pleasantness and simplicity of the trip, apparently being much impressed with the good roads and comfortable vehicle which he drove. His story usually began with, "I got up before breakfast, put my grazin's [a box of rolls] on the seat beside me, and just drove along down to Independence without a bit of trouble."

He spoke so rapidly that many people could not catch what he was saying, which on some occasions was perhaps fortunate, for his vocabulary reflected the rodeo environment in which he spent much of his life. I'm sure some who attended religious retreats and felt kindly toward him were spared a shock simply because of the rapidity of his speech. They often just didn't know what he was saying.

One day in the late sixties I was scheduled to teach a class at a ministers' gathering at Romoca. As I prepared for my presentation I looked around for a short piece of rope to use in an illustration, and sought the help of the ubiquitous Irby in obtaining one. He took me to his pickup, with its ever present load of day-old bread, dug around in his gear, and came up with a length which I could use. He seemed most pleased when I told him it was just what I needed, and I soon found him in his usual place on the front row at the extreme left as I faced the audience. He followed every word, and seemed to be especially pleased with the point I made by untwisting the rope at one end to illustrate how much stronger we are together than when each of us acts separately. After the service he came up to me and in his rapid-fire manner said, "Either we're both wrong or we're both right, because I sure as hell agree with you."

One day in the fall of 1967 I was presiding at a conference of the Denver District, which was being held in the church on Marion Street. Irby was in his usual place on the front row, and at one point in the proceedings a motion was introduced recommending the approval of certain ordinations. One of those recommended was a young man in whom Irby was interested. As opportunity for discussion was given, Irby rose to his feet and said, "This man comes from good stock. I've knowed him since he was a pup. And I knowed his folks too. He's got a good wife, too. If you've got a good wife, you've got somethin'. And if you ain't got a good wife, you've got somethin'." Needless to say, the recommendation was approved.

FROM HARRY HIGHLAND

My first recollection of Brother Irby dates back to the early 1920s. I was a lad at the time and, having lived in western Oklahoma prior to moving to Independence, I was very much impressed by his appearance which to me symbolized "the old West."

My wife, the former Mayme Beckett, recalls meeting this great cowboy at the first General Conference held in the still unfinished Auditorium. Brother Irby had brought a truckload of Saints to the Conference from Colorado. She was with a group of young people who had "trucked" in from the Holden Stake. Irby walked over to their truck as it pulled up and parked near the Auditorium and handed each of them a new shiny dime as they scrambled off the vehicle. This was indicative of his deep affection for youth. He never outlived this love for and interest in young people.

Years later, while living in Colorado Springs, we became more intimately associated with Brother Irby. He attended every activity held at the church, from women's meetings to district conferences. He was invariably "down in front" sitting in the first row. On conclusion of the service he never remained inside mingling with the members; instead he would be in front of the church handing out candy kisses to the children as they came out or passed by the church. On more than one occasion he was seen running after youngsters who chanced to be passing by our church on their way home from some other denomination. Irby would share his inexhaustible supply of candy kisses and invite the children to come to our Sunday school. He followed this same routine when attending district functions in Denver.

I recall how much he loved our small daughter, Shirley. Years later, after we had moved to the northwest, whenever we chanced to meet Irby his first question would be, "How's that little curly-headed daughter of yours?" The fact that she was married and had children of her own did not matter. His question was always the same.

On one such occasion—after we had been living in the state of Washington several years and were back in Colorado visiting church friends—Irby, in his machine-gun style of talking, asked, "Where you living now...in Spokane did you say?" I told him that was right, although I was working throughout the Spokane District. He looked at me a moment and then, half to himself and half to me, he said, "Spokane. . . Colfax, Colfax, that's the place! I'll never forget Colfax, Washington. I was riding in a rodeo there one time, and just as I came out to the chute after my calf my horse fell dead from a heart attack. I'll never forget Colfax."

I'm quite sure it was while we were living in Colorado Springs that we were told of the following incident that occurred during the Depression years. Irby was attending a dinner in Independence in the old dining hall behind the Stone Church. President Fred M. Smith, a very close friend, was to be the speaker. It seems Brother Irby had noticed the somewhat frayed cuffs on the prophet's suit coat, and during the address Irby managed to slip a hundred-dollar bill under his plate. When F. M. returned to his seat he noticed the corner of the bill protruding from beneath his plate. He raised it up, saw what it was, and, without a word, looked across the table at Irby, who merely returned his message in like silent manner.

Brother Irby used this means often to help purchase clothing befitting the office of the prophet. However, he would have reacted in the same manner, no doubt, had he found anyone in need. That was Brother Irby.

He was a champion in more ways than one. Those of us who were privileged to know him are better for the experience. What finer monument could a person leave when his mortal era is completed?

FROM GEORGE MESLEY

Irby Mundy was the essence of kindness.

After his retirement from rodeo competition he spent many years and dollars helping other cowboys ride in the roundups and achieve their own successes.

He never met a stranger in his life. He had the capacity to make friends immediately.

He had a lifelong dedication to the objectives of the church and a sound knowledge of its teachings.

FROM MRS. JAMES E. WELCH

We have many happy memories of Irby. When I was small he would frequently come to see us (we were the only church members in that area). He came one year to tell us about the youth camp being held on his property in Colorado Springs, and he encouraged my sister and me to attend. Mother took us and stayed to work in the kitchen. This was the first time we had had the opportunity to associate with so many church youth. It was a wonderful experience for us.

After James and I married Irby continued to come to see us and always encouraged us to attend church. In 1954 when he suggested that we attend World Conference we told him we just didn't have time. Then he pointed out in his colorful language that people much busier than we were going. He made it sound so wonderful we decided to attend—and he was right! Since then we have missed only two Conferences.

Irby often would send an envelope full of cards for me to give to people. He joked about not letting the post office get the money. His addressing of letters was unique. Once he sent one "Veet, Veet Reta...and pretty too. Southwest of Demmett, Taxes." Surprisingly, I received it.

I remember Irby giving me candy when I was a small girl; later he gave our children candy. They looked forward to seeing him as much as we did.

Irby would load his pickup with day-old bread and pastries in Colorado and head for Texas, stopping along the way to share the bakery goods with people. At district conference, between services he would give all the children candy. During services he always sat on the front row. How we miss seeing him there!

We loved Irby Mundy! Many of our happiest experiences originated with his encouraging us to attend church. He always bore his testimony to us, and we appreciated it.

FROM MALCOLM BARROWS

I met Irby Mundy in 1941 while I was stationed at Sheppard AFB, Wichita Falls, Texas. He would load his pickup truck with old copies of the *Herald*, fruit and cookies for his meals, and spend months at a time visiting nonresident Saints in Oklahoma, Texas, Eastern Colorado, etc. He seldom would accept an invitation to stay in anyone's home, preferring to get on "down the line" to the next stop. When he got tired he would sleep in the cab of his pickup truck.

On rare occasions when he did sleep in a home, he would say before retiring, "Don't bother about getting me any breakfast." Usually he would get up quietly at 3:00 or 4:00 a.m. and depart.

His last big time performance (calf-roping, milking a wild cow, bulldogging, etc.) was at Frontier Days in

Cheyenne in 1946. I attended the last day after Irby had been eliminated from the finals. He was fifty-eight years old at the time and decided his competition days were over. He did, however, continue to follow the rodeos, selling cowboy boots, hats, etc. His wife, Jewel, went with him and worked in the concession stand.

Irby's prize money during his prime riding years may be of interest. Just a few months before his first stroke late in 1971 he mailed me three sale bills of the eight-day rodeo in Madison Square Garden in New York City held in 1933. Irby entered three events: calf-roping, milking a wild cow, and bulldogging... and took first place in all three. His total prize money at this one meet was about $33,000. Cowboys who did not win would "borrow" money from Irby. So, at the end of his career, he had only limited savings laid aside. I understand that his brother who lived in the panhandle of Texas and had extensive land interests helped Irby along in his later life and bought him a new pickup about every two years.

During the year Irby was in the rest home in Colorado Springs occasionally people would hand his wife or daughter some money to help out with his expenses. Dorothy, who hesitated to accept such contributions, had difficulty holding back tears of joy when nice things were done for her father.

Irby was baptized in a stock tank. Several others were baptized also, and Irby was last in line. Just before stepping up to the tank, he flipped a cigarette from his mouth. Afterwards he said to Brother J. D. Curtis, "I notice that the Saints don't smoke. Would it be better if I didn't?" Brother Curtis explained the church stand on the use of tobacco, and Irby said, "I'm quitting right now. I want to be the best Saint possible."

And what a worker he was! Until he was in his late seventies very few could keep up with him. But he appreciated the esthetic as well as the physical.

It is a matter of record that he was present at the *Messiah* presentation for fifty-three consecutive years.

When I ask myself what Irby has done for me, I have to reply that he has inspired me to want to continue faithful in my life and ministry. I hope I can be as useful to my fellowmen as Irby was. He will ever be a challenge to me as he was to thousands of others.

FROM ERNEST E. CROWNOVER

Both Muriel and I knew Irby well from our childhood. I kept in contact with him until his last days. Our memories of him are like those of thousands of other people: his visits with the Saints, his inexhaustible supply of candy kisses, his rapid speech, his presence at church activities, and his concern for people. I never heard him speak an ill word to or of anyone.

I could mention very little that is not also a part of recollections of everyone who knew him. I deeply regret that I did not retain some of the many postcards we received from him, and that we did not have the foresight to record his voice.

FROM F. HENRY EDWARDS

I was a guest in the Mundy home in Utleyville, Colorado, when the Utleyville branch was organized. I had never ridden a horse, and Irby got me astride his "paint pony," put a rope in my hand, and held my attention while a picture was taken. Thereafter, his letters were always addressed to "Cowboy Edwards."

My wife and Irby and Jewell were very good friends. Not very many years ago when she was in Colorado Springs she went to Wednesday prayer service with Irby. Then, after the meeting was over, Irby rushed her out to the track, because she had never seen a dog race.

When the children were small they loved to have Irby visit. More than once he took them behind the scenes at the circus.

I offended Irby once. He was generous to a fault, and it seemed to Alice and me that people sometimes took advantage. He bought several bedspreads at some church sale and gave them to Alice's friends before he saw her. He apologized for having no spread for her, and said he would get one. I remonstrated that we did not need this to cement our friendship, and I must have expressed myself awkwardly. He went off in high indignation saying, "No spread for *your* bed!" Later Alice found what had happened and explained the situation to him. The next thing I knew he had bought her a Mexican serape.

Irby was a good man and a fine friend.

Conclusion

If there is calf-roping in that great beyond, I know where Irby Mundy will be when the chute is opened. If there are animals, or ropes, or saddles there, I know Irby will have a collection of them already. How do I know this? Because I believe Irby was right when he told me that what a man is by choice in this life rises out of his inner soul.

Irby was a cowboy by choice augmented by a one hundred percent desire to be the best cowboy in the world. I think he succeeded. It took such dedication as this to carry him to two world championships and the respect of thousands of admirers. I doubt that I will ever look upon a wholesome western scene without thinking of my good friend Irby.

Irby was indeed predictable. It was the simple quality that endeared him to all. For this reason I think I can hear the echo of his words as he rode over the crest of that last high hill:

"Don't have pity on me, Notorious Ed. Well past ambush, country-golden daylight ahead. Prettiest white horse I ever saw. If silver lariats are as good as the rope I used to lasso Happy, I've got the horse I've been chasing since I was a pup.... Never had the heart to tell you before. You'll never be a good cowboy—too thick on the east side goin' west. Don't give up, though; I saw a fat, lame ox before the divide. Believe you could catch him. So long for now; got to be moseying on. Looks like a fantastic roundup ahead.

"Adios!"